DREAM JOBS
If You Like
KIDS

by Amie Jane Leavitt

CAPSTONE PRESS
a capstone imprint

Capstone Captivate is published by Capstone Press, an imprint of Capstone.
1710 Roe Crest Drive
North Mankato, Minnesota 56003
www.capstonepub.com

Copyright © 2021 by Capstone. All rights reserved. No part of this publication may be reproduced in whole or in part, or stored in a retrieval system, or transmitted in any form or by any means, electronic, mechanical, photocopying, recording, or otherwise, without written permission of the publisher.

Library of Congress Cataloging-in-Publication Data is available on the Library of Congress website.
ISBN: 978-1-4966-8398-4 (library binding)
ISBN: 978-1-4966-8449-3 (eBook PDF)

Summary: Wouldn't it be cool to have a job working with or around the things you love? Do you enjoy helping people? Maybe a career in pediatrics is something you would care for! Readers will discover the possibilities of careers working with kids.

Image Credits
iStockphoto: FatCamera, 12, Hispanolistic, 19, kate_sept2004, back cover, 7, Morsa Images, 8; Pixabay: TheDigitalArtist, (lines) Cover; Shutterstock: Happy Max, 11, Ho Su A Bi, 21, Iakov Filimonov, 15, michaeljung, 5, MIKHAIL GRACHIKOV, (dots) Cover, Monkey Business Images, 28, 29, New Africa, 16, Rawpixel.com, 14, StockImageFactory.com, Cover, Tyler Olson, 26, vlas2000, 25, wavebreakmedia, 23

Editorial Credits
Editor: Heather Williams; Designer: Sara Radka; Media Researcher: Morgan Walters; Production Specialist: Spencer Rosio

All internet sites appearing in back matter were available and accurate when this book was sent to press.

Printed in the United States
PA117

Table of Contents

Pediatrician 4

Babysitter or Nanny 6

Neonatal Nurse 8

Newborn and Child Photographer 10

Child Day Care Worker 12

Coach 14

Child Psychologist 16

Pediatric Physical Therapist..................... 18

Child Entertainer... 20

Elementary School Teacher 22

Pediatric Dentistry 24

Children's Librarian 26

Museum Educator 28

    Glossary 30

    Read More 31

    Internet Sites 31

    Index 32

Words in **bold** are in the glossary.

What would it be like to take pictures of kids all day? What if your job were to care for babies in a hospital? You might want to consider one of these careers for your future. One could end up being your dream job!

Pediatrician

Kids have their own special doctors. These doctors are called **pediatricians**. They work with kids up until the age of 18. These doctors work in clinics and hospitals. They work with sick and well children.

On the Job

Many pediatricians start their day at the hospital. They visit their patients. Some patients are ill. Others might have had surgery. Then the doctors go to their offices. They meet with patients who have appointments. They do "well visits," checking children who are not sick. They give shots. They make sure the child is growing properly. Pediatricians also see sick children. They try to figure out why they're sick. Then they might write **prescriptions** to help the children get better.

> **FUN FACT**
>
> There are 15 different kinds of pediatricians. Each has a unique area of focus. **Pediatric cardiologists** work with kids who have heart problems. Pediatric pulmonologists help children with lung problems.

Going to the doctor for a checkup can be a fun experience!

Pay Range

Average salary for a general pediatrician is between $174,000 and $239,000 per year. Salaries are generally higher for those who have specialties.

Education and Skills

Pediatricians go to college for at least eight years. First they study a subject such as biology. Then they go to medical school. Next they do a **residency**. During a residency, new doctors learn from doctors who have experience. Pediatricians must love working with kids. They should know about health and nutrition too. Doctors go to classes and read articles. Things change often in the medical field. Doctors need to know the latest information. This allows them to best help their patients.

Babysitter or Nanny

Who gets called when parents need to go out for the evening? The babysitter, of course. Who gets hired to care for children while the parents are at work? That is usually the job of a nanny. Babysitters work only a few hours every so often. Nannies work full- or part-time for families.

On the Job

Babysitters and nannies care for kids when the parents are not there. They make sure the children are safe. They also do fun things with the kids. They watch TV programs or movies. They play games. Sometimes they make food for the children. Other times they drive kids to school or sports practice. Nannies sometimes live in the family's home. They might do light cleaning. Babysitters usually just care for the children. Some families bring nannies along on trips. Nannies take care of the children just like they do at home.

Pay Range

Pay varies for babysitters. For nannies it ranges between $26,000 and $36,000 per year.

Education and Skills

Most babysitters and nannies have special skills. They like to spend many hours with children. They are also creative. They can come up with fun activities for children to do. Nannies and babysitters often know **first aid**. This helps them if children get hurt. The Red Cross offers babysitting classes. Parents often want their babysitters to have first-aid training.

FUN FACT

Nannies can work in unusual places. Some work on cruise ships or hotels. Others work for airlines.

Even though nannies help with mealtime and bedtime, playtime is important too!

Neonatal Nurse

A neonatal nurse cares for babies who are born early. These babies are very small. Sometimes they are born with health problems. These nurses also care for babies with physical challenges.

Neonatal nurses check on babies in the NICU many times each day.

On the Job

Neonatal nurses work in the Neonatal Intensive Care Unit (NICU). It is a special part of the hospital. Babies get extra care there. Neonatal nurses watch a baby's heart rate and breathing. They also give the baby food. Babies might need a feeding tube. Or they might take a bottle. The nurses measure the baby's length and weight. They record everything about the baby on a chart. A doctor reviews these notes to make sure the baby is growing. Babies can go home with their families when they are healthy enough.

> **FUN FACT**
> Up to 21 million babies around the world are born with low birth weight every year. Some tiny babies are born at 23 weeks and are as small as 1 pound (454 grams).

Pay Range

Average salary = $60,000 per year.

Education and Skills

Neonatal nurses go to school for two to four years. They must pass a special test. It shows that they have the knowledge and skills needed to work with babies. Nurses work long hours. They are on their feet most of the time. Nurses must be good at science. They should also be organized. They must pay close attention to detail.

Newborn and Child Photographer

Parents love to have photos of their children. They display them on their walls and desks. It can be hard to get good pictures of babies and children. A special photographer can get just the right shot.

On the Job

Newborn and child photographers often work with **props**. These can include small chairs, cradles, baskets, buckets, and bowls. Photographers often have fun clothes for the children to wear. Some photographers take photos in their own studio. Others go to the family's home. Some even work outside. Photographers use many tricks to keep children happy and smiling. They bring toys and stuffed animals. These help get the child's attention. They might also speak in silly voices and make funny faces. They try many things to make the child laugh.

Pay Range

Average salary = $34,000 per year. It could be much less or much more, depending upon the talent and marketing skills of the photographer.

Child photographers look for unique props and settings to create the best photos.

Education and Skills

Some photographers go to college. They study photography. Others learn as a hobby. Then they turn it into a job. Photographers must know how to use all kinds of equipment. They use digital cameras. Sometimes they need special lights. Many photographers edit their photos. They use computer software. Newborn and baby photographers must have a fun personality. They must bring out the best in children. Child photographers should also be creative. They need to set up a scene with just the right props and clothing.

FUN FACT

Anne Geddes is one of the most famous baby photographers in the world. She takes pictures of babies in unusual places. Some babies are placed in flower pots. Some are dressed up like bees. Others are nestled in pumpkin patches.

Child Day Care Worker

Many kids go to day care centers when their parents are at work. Large day care centers have many children and workers. Small centers are often found in people's homes. They might have only a few children and one or two workers. Some centers offer preschool for young kids. Many have after-school programs for older children.

Story time is a fun part of day care for many young children.

On the Job

Day care center workers have many tasks to do each day. Their most important job is caring for the children. They make sure the children eat on time. They make sure they stay safe. The workers also change diapers and rock babies to sleep. They try to make the day fun for children. They play games with them. They find toys that the children will like. Some even take kids on field trips or to the park. They teach new skills, read books, and sing songs.

> **FUN FACT**
> Some day care centers offer care for both children and senior citizens. At these centers, the two age groups do many activities together.

Pay Range

Average salary = $24,000 per year.

Education and Skills

Day care workers usually learn on the job. They are trained by workers with more experience. Day care center workers should have basic child-care skills. They should know how to calm upset children, feed them, and change their diapers. They should also know first aid in case a child gets hurt. Some day care center workers are teachers. They lead the preschool and after-school programs at the centers.

Coaches teach young players about game skills, teamwork, and how to be a good sport.

Coach

What do golf, gymnastics, soccer, and basketball have in common? Coaches! Coaches help train players and teams of all ages. They lead the way at practices and games. They are hired by cities and community centers. Coaches also work for private studios and schools.

On the Job

Coaches teach players the rules of the sport. They help them improve their skills. Some coaches work with one athlete all day long. Some work with many different groups of athletes at different times of the day. Other coaches work with teams after school or on weekends. Coaches can work in just one sport or many sports.

Pay Range

Between $23,000 and $53,000 per year, depending on where the person is coaching. Coaches for city sports may get paid less. Some coach for free.

Education and Skills

Some coaches go to college. They might study fitness, physical education, or sports medicine. Coaches must know the sport they are leading. They must know the rules. They are also good teachers. They have to teach athletes how to best play the sport. They can learn on the job. They are often former athletes. But that is not required. Great coaches can teach others even if they have never played the sport themselves.

FUN FACT
About 35 million children play youth sports every season in the United States.

Gymnasts usually work with one coach for many hours at a time each day.

Child Psychologist

Some parts of life can be tough for children. School can cause a lot of **stress**. Parents sometimes get divorced. Loved ones pass away. Child psychologists help children learn how to handle all kinds of difficult moments. They teach kids **coping skills** that will help them throughout their lives.

A child psychologist can help kids talk about tough issues and find ways to get through hard times.

On the Job

Child psychologists work with individual kids and groups. They first find out the problem the kids are facing. Then they decide the best treatment plan. They give the children daily tasks to work on. They might give kids ways to calm down when they are stressed or anxious. The children talk about how they did on these tasks at their next **session**. A child psychologist's main goal is to help kids learn how to help themselves.

FUN FACT
Music **therapy** is one way that child psychologists can help young children. It can help calm children who feel anxious. It can also help children manage stress.

Pay Range

Average salary = $78,000 per year.

Education and Skills

Child psychologists go to college for six to eight years. They study child development or psychology. People who do well in this job are good listeners. They understand people's feelings. They like to help others. They are trustworthy. Children must feel they can trust their psychologist. Psychologists should never talk about their patients' problems to others.

Pediatric Physical Therapist

Sometimes children have problems with their bodies. Maybe they were born with a disability. Or they broke a bone while playing a sport. These kids are treated by a doctor first. Then they go to a pediatric physical therapist. These people know a lot about the human body and how it moves. They help children learn to move and complete daily tasks.

On the Job

Pediatric physical therapists take a look at a child's physical challenges. They study **X-rays** and read doctors' notes. Then they make a treatment plan. Some pediatric physical therapists work with kids in schools or in kids' homes. Others work in hospitals or offices. The therapist has certain equipment for the patient to use. Some examples are bouncy balls, walking machines, and mini-skateboards. This equipment helps strengthen muscles and improve body movement. Pediatric physical therapists include families and caretakers in the sessions. They show them how to help the patient between visits.

Pay Range

Average salary = $65,000 per year.

Education and Skills

Pediatric physical therapists go to college for six to eight years. Most take classes in anatomy and physical therapy. They pay attention to details. They know how the body works. They understand proper body movement. These therapists can give instructions clearly. They are also patient. They want to help others improve their lives through physical movement.

FUN FACT

Polio is a disease that can cause **paralysis**. Today, a shot keeps people from getting the disease. In the early 1900s, thousands of people got the disease. The field of pediatric physical therapy was developed to help polio victims.

Pediatric physical therapists work one-on-one with their patients.

Child Entertainer

A magician surprises kids with card tricks. A balloon artist makes animals out of colorful balloons. A costumed cartoon character marches in a parade and poses for pictures at theme parks. These examples all describe a day in the life of a child entertainer.

On the Job

Child entertainers sometimes have their own business. They can be hired for birthday parties and special events. Or they can be the star at a community event. They work at carnivals and festivals. Some work for big theme parks. They dress up like well-known cartoon or movie characters. They spend the day singing and dancing. They march in parades and meet guests. Child entertainers can take on many roles. They can be magicians and balloon artists. They can be fairies and princesses. They can be clowns and puppeteers. They can even be traveling scientists who do fun experiments. Jugglers and face painters entertain children too.

Pay Range

Salary varies widely and depends on many factors. The average is about $60,000 per year but could be much less or much more.

Many child entertainers use bright colors and funny costumes to keep kids laughing.

Education and Skills

Many child entertainers learn on the job. They learn from other entertainers. They study videos or instructions online. Or they get trained by the companies that hire them. Many entertainers use skills and talents they already have. Someone who juggles can dress up like a clown and become a child entertainer. People who make fun shapes out of balloons can market themselves as a balloon artist.

FUN FACT

Blippi is a children's entertainer. He started out dressing up as a character to entertain his nephew. Then he started a YouTube channel. He is now a millionaire!

Elementary School Teacher

Elementary school teachers work with children. They teach kindergarten through fifth or sixth grade. They often teach all subjects. They work in public schools, charter schools, and private schools. They might also work with students one-on-one at tutoring centers.

On the Job

Elementary teachers make lesson plans for every subject they teach. They write down the materials they need. Then they decide how to teach the lessons. Teachers create classroom management plans. They decide how they want the students to behave in their class. They might create a reward system using colors. Teachers also try to make sure their classrooms are fun places for learning. They hang interesting posters and design bulletin boards. They set up classroom libraries and art centers. The teacher is not finished when the school day ends. Tests need to be graded. Lesson plans must be written. Teachers often work many long hours preparing for their students.

FUN FACT

An online company in China employs 70,000 teachers to teach English online to 600,000 Chinese students. The teachers do this from the comfort of their own homes!

Pay Range

Between $32,000 and $79,000 per year.

Education and Skills

Elementary school teachers must go to college for at least four years. Many must pass a special test. People in this job usually have many skills. They know about many subjects. Teachers like working with kids. They enjoy helping them learn new topics. They have patience. They are usually creative people. Every student learns differently. Teachers must think of many ways to teach the same topic.

Elementary school teachers can help kids learn about many subjects, from reading to math to art.

Pediatric Dentistry

Some dentists' offices focus only on young patients. The workers in these offices care for children's teeth and gums as they change. They treat issues that are unique to growing teeth. They know that some kids are scared of going to the dentist's office. The dentists and other workers help these young patients have a good experience.

On the Job

Many people work at pediatric dentists' offices. Pediatric dentists have a staff of people who work with young children. Dental assistants help the dentists. They take X-rays. They clean tools and get supplies. Dental hygienists clean teeth. They use special tools to remove buildup on teeth. They use other tools to polish and clean the teeth. Dentists look at X-rays. They help pull baby teeth that are loose. They check for cavities. These are small holes in the teeth. They can be caused by sugar or by not cleaning your teeth well. Orthodontists are special kinds of dentists. They put braces on teeth. Braces straighten teeth. Braces also correct the way the teeth fit together in the mouth.

FUN FACT
Tooth enamel is the hardest substance in the human body.

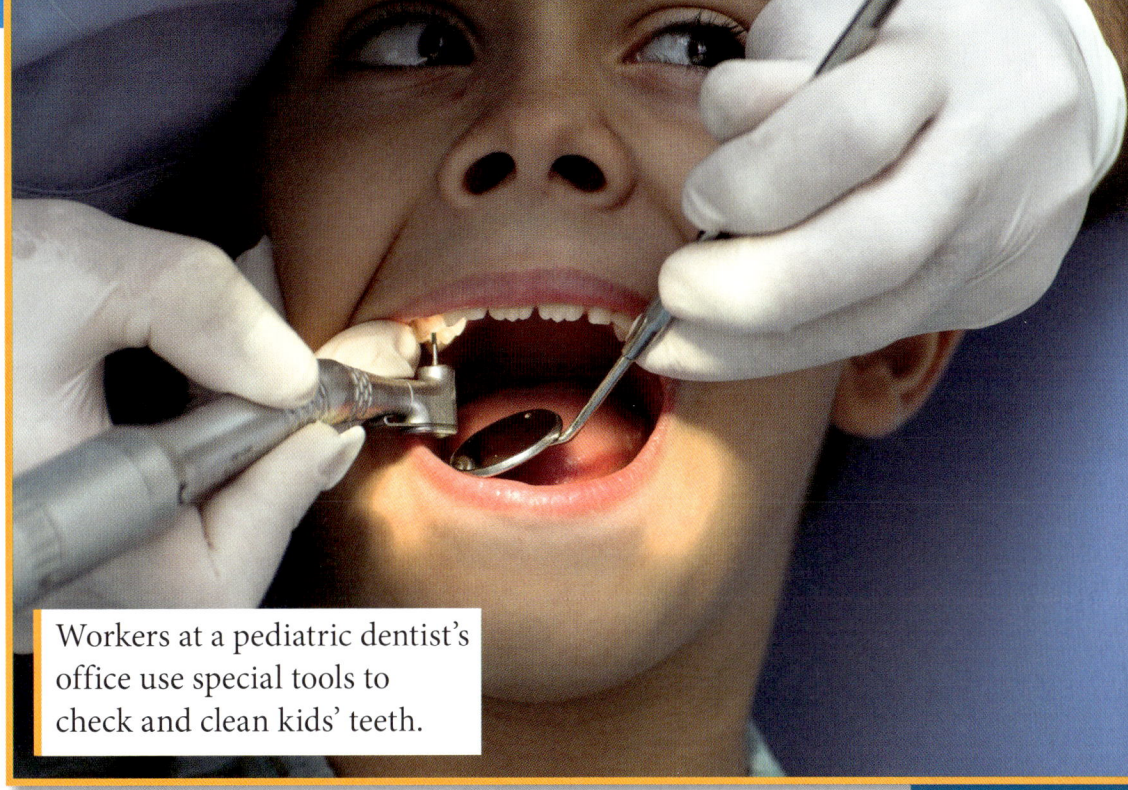

Workers at a pediatric dentist's office use special tools to check and clean kids' teeth.

Pay Range

Salaries vary. Dental assistants make the least, around $38,000 per year. Dental hygienists make about $75,000 per year. Pediatric dentists make about $175,000 per year. Orthodontists make an average of $226,000 per year.

Education and Skills

Dental assistants usually need only a high school diploma. They learn on the job. Dental hygienists go to school for two to four years. Dentists complete at least eight years of college. Orthodontists also complete at least eight years of college. They take special classes in orthodontics too.

Children's Librarian

Libraries are not just places where books are stored. They are also places where people come to learn in fun and creative ways. Children's librarians are a big part of the fun. They plan special events based on books. They also hold camps and after-school programs. Kids can learn computer coding or complete art projects at these events.

Librarians are skilled at helping every reader find just the right story.

On the Job

Children's librarians wear many hats. They put away books. They read new books so they can recommend them to readers. They plan story times. They help kids use computers and show them how to check out electronic books. Sometimes librarians work with members of the community, such as doctors or policemen. These people give talks at the library. Children's librarians often must raise money for their library. They hold used book sales or book fairs.

> **FUN FACT**
> Some children's book authors started their careers as children's librarians! One of them is Beverly Cleary. She created the well-known characters Beezus and Ramona.

Pay Range

Average salary = $51,000 per year.

Education and Skills

Many children's librarians go to college for four to six years. They study library science. Those who do not go to college learn on the job. All librarians must be organized. They must also like researching topics. Kids and adults often come to them with questions. Librarians may need to research to find the answers.

Museum Educator

Teachers don't just work at schools. They also work in all kinds of museums. Some work in art museums. Others work at science centers. Some work at history museums. Others work at children's discovery centers. Teachers have a special job to do at all of these places. They help visitors learn about a variety of topics.

On the Job

Museum educators have many jobs. Sometimes they help put together exhibits. They look at a collection of items. Then they decide which ones would be most interesting to display. They often write signs that tell visitors why these objects are important. Museum educators may show guests how things work. They might talk about a piece of art. They might show an animal and tell why it is unique. Some museum educators plan camps and overnight events at the museum too.

Hands-on exhibits are memorable parts of many museums.

Pay Range

Between $38,000 and $69,000 per year.

Education and Skills

Most museum educators go to college. They study education. Or they study a specific subject like art or science. Those who do not have a degree learn on the job. They might start out as a regular employee. They might have other jobs in the museum. Then they learn how to lead talks. They learn how to plan events. Museum educators should enjoy teaching. They should also like to learn. They will spend a lot of time learning about new topics. Speaking, listening, reading, and writing skills are important.

FUN FACT

Museums spend more than $2 billion each year on educational activities. The typical museum spends three-fourths of its education budget on K–12 students.

People who work at museums know many facts about a number of subjects.

Glossary

coping skill (KOH-ping SKILL)—a method a person uses to deal with problems

first aid (FUHRST AYD)—the help given to a person with a minor or serious medical issue

paralysis (puh-RA-lih-siss)—loss of movement of all or some of the body

pediatric (pee-dee-A-trik)—involving children

pediatrician (pee-dee-uh-TRI-shun)—a doctor who cares for babies and children

prescription (pri-SKRIP-shun)—an order for medicine from a doctor

prop (PRAHP)—an item used by a photographer during a photo session

residency (REZ-uh-den-see)—time of advanced training with an experienced doctor that takes place after medical school

session (SESH-uhn)—an amount of time

stress (STRESS)—the body's way of reacting to physical, emotional, or mental factors

therapy (THER-uh-pee)—a treatment for an illness, an injury, or a disability

X-ray (EKS-ray)—a photograph of the inside of a person's body

Read More

Giovinco, Gerry. *The Big Book of Balloon Art: More Than 100 Fun Sculptures.* Mineola, NY: Dover Publications, 2019.

Jacquart, Anne-Laure. *Photo Adventures for Kids: Solving the Mysteries of Taking Great Photos.* San Rafael, CA: Rocky Nook, 2016.

Reilly, Kathleen M., and Alexis Cornell. *The Human Body: Get Under the Skin With Science Activities For Kids.* White River Junction, VT: Nomad Press, 2019.

Wall, Matthew. *So You Want to Learn Juggling?* Lincoln, NE: Handersen Publishing LLC, 2017.

Wilson, Becky. *Sticker World – Museum.* Lonely Planet Kids. Oakland, CA: Lonely Planet, 2018.

Internet Sites

Children's Dental Care
https://kidshealth.org/en/kids/go-dentist.html

Learn How to Juggle
https://www.thejugglingscientist.com/learn-to-juggle.html

Learn How to Puppeteer!
https://www.jimhensonsfamilyhub.com/home-1/2017/8/31/learn-how-to-puppeteer

Index

art, 22, 26, 28, 29

babysitters, 6–7

child development, 17
child entertainers, 20–21
coaches, 14–15
creativity, 7, 11, 23, 26

day care worker, 12–13
dentistry, 24–25

first aid, 7, 13
food, 6, 9, 13

Geddes, Anne, 11

health, 5, 8

librarians, 26–27

museum educators, 28–29

nannies, 6–7
neonatal nurses, 8–9
nutrition, 5

organization, 9, 27

pediatricians, 4–5
photographer, 10–11
physical therapists, 18–19
planning, 17, 18, 26, 27, 28, 29
psychologists, 16–17

science, 9, 27, 28, 29
sports, 6, 14, 15, 18

teachers, 22–23